leapfrog
Learners

Knights

by Annabelle Lynch

W
FRANKLIN WATTS
LONDON • SYDNEY

First published in 2013 by
Franklin Watts
338 Euston Road
London
NW1 3BH

Franklin Watts Australia
Level 17/207 Kent Street
Sydney, NSW 2000

Copyright © Franklin Watts 2013

Picture credits: Tomasz Bidermann/Shutterstock: 21.
Robert Creigh/istockphoto: front cover, 12. Istvan Csak/Shutterstock: 6.
Kilukilu/Shutterstock: 11. Lebrecht Music & Arts/Alamy: 16.
Richard T. Nowitz/Corbis: 15. Private Collection/Index/BAL: 5.
Raulin/Shutterstock: 18-19. Gustavo Tomsich/Corbis: 8.

Every attempt has been made to clear copyright.
Should there be any inadvertent omission please
apply to the publisher for rectification.

A CIP catalogue record for this book is
available from the British Library.

Dewey number: 940.1

ISBN 978 1 4451 1646 4 (hbk)
ISBN 978 1 4451 1652 5 (pbk)
Library eBook ISBN 978 1 4451 2549 7

Series Editor: Julia Bird
Picture Researcher: Diana Morris
Series Advisor: Catherine Glavina
Series Designer: Peter Scoulding

Franklin Watts is a division of Hachette Children's Books,
an Hachette UK company.
www.hachette.co.uk

Contents

The words in **bold** can be found in the glossary.

What was a knight?

Knights were **soldiers** who lived hundreds of years ago. They worked for a king or **lord**.

A king made a man a knight by touching him on the shoulder with a sword.

6

Becoming a knight

Boys **trained** to become a knight from the age of seven. They learned how to fight with weapons and how to ride a horse.

A young knight was called a squire.

Into battle!

Knights fought in
battles to defend
their lord or king's land,
or to win new land.

Knights rode horses
into battle.

Armour

In battle, knights wore a metal **suit of armour**. This protected them against blows from the enemy's weapons.

Armour was very heavy to wear!

Weapons

Knights carried many weapons to defend them. These included a **lance**, sword and **battle-axe**.

Knights used long lances to charge at the enemy on horseback.

Jousting

Knights got ready for battle at **jousting** games. Two knights charged at each other with a lance, trying to knock the other off his horse!

Knights who won jousts got a big prize of money.

Chivalry

All knights were meant to behave well. This was called **chivalry**. They had to be brave, act kindly and keep their promises.

Knights promised to protect women.

Crusades

Knights went on long journeys called **crusades**. They went to protect **Christianity** and to take over new lands.

Crusades could last for many years.

See for yourself!

Today, people dress up as knights and have pretend battles. Why not go and see one for yourself?

Pretend battles can be exciting to watch!

Glossary

Battle – a fight between enemies

Battle-axe – a big axe with a wide head

Chivalry – rules of how a knight should behave

Christianity – a religion that follows the teachings of Jesus Christ

Crusades – when knights went to other countries to protect Christianity and win new lands

Jousting – fighting on horseback with a lance

Lance – a long weapon with a pointed head

Lord – a man who had a lot of land and money

Soldiers – people in the army

Suit of armour – a metal outfit that covers the body

Train – to learn special skills

Website:

http://www.activityvillage.co.uk/knights_theme.htm

Every effort has been made by the Publishers to ensure that the websites are suitable for children, and that they contain no inappropriate or offensive material. However, because of the nature of the Internet, it is impossible to guarantee that the contents of these sites will not be altered. We strongly advise that Internet access is supervised by a responsible adult.

Quiz

Use the information in the book to answer these questions.

1. Who did knights work for?

2. At what age did boys begin training to become a knight?

3. Why did knights wear armour?

4. What animal did knights ride when they were jousting?

5. How long could crusades last?

(The answers are on page 24.)

Answers

1. A king or a lord
2. Seven
3. To protect them from blows from the enemy's weapons
4. Horse
5. Many years

Index